IRON
HORSE

ISBN 978-1-945028-35-9

Published by St. Vitus Dance
please visit STVITUS.DANCE

THEMIKESANPEDRO@PROTONMAIL.COM

BOOK ONE

IRON HORSE

100 DAYS OF TIMELESS WISDOM

To Help You Go the Distance Against Yourself, Your Adversaries, and the Misfortunes of Life

M. SAN PEDRO

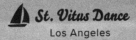 St. Vitus Dance
Los Angeles

To EJG, you are the friend that sticks closer
than a brother. +25 years and counting.

To BVO, your dedication to philosophy and knowledge is something I envy.

HOW TO READ THIS BOOK:

This book was burst out of the pain, confusion, lack of direction and mistakes that I made in my life. It's everything I wish I had known growing up. While these words and thoughts are mine, they are rooted in the timeless wisdom of Seneca, Epictetus, the Japanese Ronin Miyamoto Musashi, Emperors Napoleon Bonaparte, Caesar, and Marcus Aurelius, and my personal favorite, who will remain nameless. Some of these truths you will like, some you will wish you never had to use, and some you'll hate. But I promise you they will all serve you in your time of need: when your mind is getting the best of you, when you are on a roller coaster of emotions, or when your adversaries are seeking to destroy you in the corporate world. It will serve you most of all when you are engulfed by the misfortunes of life.

This book is designed to give you the mental endurance of a thoroughbred.

It is important for us to see things as they are and not as we would like them to be. This book is meant to condition your mind and strengthen your spirit. It is designed to give you the mental endurance of a thoroughbred, so you can go the distance against the harsh realities of life.

The truths found in this book should not be used offensively, nor to manipulate. They are to be use defensively and to aid.

These maxims are short—as they should be. For what is true should be short and easily said. The bottom portion of each page is for you to reflect on what you have read. Write down your thoughts as to how each daily truth relates to you any particular situation you have been in, past or the present—and most certainly the future.

One page per day. Meditating on what you have read and allowing it to ruminate in your mind. It is a small investment with a large return.

All my Best,
MSP
THEMIKESANPEDRO@PROTONMAIL.COM

What is true should be
short and easily said.
•••••••••••••••••••••••••••••••••••••

(Keep this in mind as
you write on each page.)

TABLE OF CONTENTS

How to Use This Book
Iron Horse
About the Author

His heart was outsized and it made him a fierce competitor; giving him strength even against God's greatest blows.

Accept everything just the way it is.

—DOKKODO 1

Write on the dotted lines

KNOW WHEN TO MOVE ... ON

••

Sometimes the only way to deal with misfortune is to forget about it.

Do everything that **you** can do. Move every mountain **you** can move. If you've done all you can and are still burdened by the problem, it's best to forget about it and move on.

Some situations don't have a solution. They are brought into your life to teach you a lesson. Learn the lesson so the pain isn't in vain, then forget about the situation.

Don't give chase to the wind.

TIME AND SPACE

••

Space you can recover, Time you cannot.

The Great Emperor, Napoleon Bonaparte, said this: *How are you spending your time?*

You can always get another job. You can always move to another city. You can always recover whatever tangibles you have lost.

But the time you are losing you can never have back.

UNDERSTAND MURPHY'S LAW

Anything that can go wrong will go wrong.

So, the less you do in a given situation and the quicker you do it, the better you neutralize this principle.

Do only what is necessary. Tend to your own garden and wait for the harvest.

If you retreat long enough, you allow Murphy's Law to make the worst come to pass... for your opposition. Everything you do should be out of calculation, not desperation.

RATION YOUR STRENGTH

• •

Strategize! Never engage a problem strength for strength. Instead, search for weakness in the problem and attack there.

A bonfire built on kindling would be a waste of wood.

Never fight a war of attrition.

THINK BEFORE YOU ACT

• •

Humanity is very impatient, and stupidity is very bold... Don't charge ahead, WAIT!

Emotions will cause you to act hastily.

Take time to ask yourself if you're *feeling* or *thinking*.

It's very important that we think about what we are thinking about. No emotion, all reason.

RAGE AGAINST THE MACHINE

• •

Do not respond to things mechanically. Every situation is different.

If you are always responding, it is out of emotion. Stop and think.

We tend to respond to situations based on our past experiences and the prejudices they have created in our subconscious.

Are you reacting out of reason, or out of the behavior patterns your past experiences have created in your mind?

PERSPECTIVE

•••

If you're always reacting, you have no perspective. You're responding based on past emotions and experience. Consider the word "reacting:" acting *again*. Make a conscious choice to not repeat the past.

Remember, between stimulus and response there is time.

Whether it's thirty seconds or thirty days, use that time to decide your next move.

THE ART OF SELF POSSESSION

....

> **"To remain calm and disciplined while** waiting for disorder to appear amongst your enemy is the art of self possession."
>
> —SUN TZU

Disorder appears naturally in a divided mind. Windows are the first things to break in a hurricane. When you let disordered emotions into your own mind, you're leaving your windows wide open in a hurricane.

Build the house of your Self on a rock-solid foundation of logic.

Let your adversity fall victim to Murphy's Law while you remain calm and disciplined, gathering resources, becoming smarter, stronger and seeking higher ground.

SHARPEN YOUR FOCUS

• •

Look beyond your current circumstance. Focus on the grand strategy.

It is easy to become discouraged when a present situation doesn't go our way.

We focus on what we see (The Present) not on the invisible (The Future).

Learn to sow future seeds of victory in your present defeat.

Do not seek pleasure for its own sake.

—DOKKODO 2

PATIENCE WINS THE WAR

Be patient and think several steps ahead. Wage a campaign instead of fighting battles.

Expecting to win every battle is like a boxer expecting to win every round. It's not realistic.

Focus on winning the fight, not each round.

LOOK AHEAD

• •

Do not look to what is most immediate. Taking the most direct route is petty thinking.

Binoculars make objects 200 feet away appear 20 feet away. Use your mental binoculars to keep your vision off of short-term rewards.

If you are looking at what is most immediate or taking the easiest way out, you are either lazy or emotional, and it will not end well for you in that particular circumstance.

REASON'S ENEMY

••

Look at your circumstances dispassionately, with no emotion.
Consider the long-term consequences of your decision.

Emotions are the enemy of reason.

Reason and moderation keep you safe.

CLIMBING A MOUNTAIN

· ·

Your daily strategy should not be emotional, linear, or reactive. Think beyond your present troubles.

Mountain climbers map their route carefully, but they must anticipate the unexpected.

Think about the end result and securing long-term victory, not whatever trouble is presently burdening your heart. The troubles of the present will pass.

DAY 14
EYES ON THE PRIZE

Forgetting your objective is the most frequent act of all stupidity. Always keep your objectives and grand strategy in the forefront of your mind.

This should consume the majority of your thoughts, the majority of the day.

Where our eyes focus is where our attention focuses. For this reason, surround yourself with greatness, so that your objective is impossible to forget. Only consume materials that will further your ultimate goal.

Do not, under any circumstances, depend on a partial feeling.

—DOKKODO 3

DAY 15
OPEN YOUR MIND'S EYE
●●●

Observation, imagination, and contemplation are your mind's biggest assets. Stupidity acts from emotion, not from the mind or intuition.

Practice extending your vision. See the future, the world around you, and always more than your enemies do.

Speak little and observe very much.

The most powerful person in the room is listening, not speaking. Everyone wonders what the quiet person is thinking.

"In quietness and confidence shall be your strength."
—THE PROPHET ISAIAH

PREPARATION OVER PRIDE

• •

Bring the war to arenas your circumstances have ignored.

The "unsinkable" Titanic could've carried 64 lifeboats, but its engineers fell victim to pride, and only included 20 lifeboats on the ship. This caused one of history's most regrettable disasters.

Where does your life lack sufficient lifeboats?

Look for the weakness in your circumstances, and in your opponent. Weakness always comes from a lack of preparation.

Always double your resources in the summer when the sun is shining so you will not lack when winter arrives.

THE CHAIN OF BATTLE

Learn to think three or four battles ahead. Battles connect like links on a chain. Individual battles only matter in the way they set up the next ones down the line.

"A chain is no stronger than its weakest link, and life is, after all, a chain."

—WILLIAM JAMES

One lost battle can be the strongest link on your chain, if you learn from your mistake.

Again, even if you see you are going to lose a present battle, be sure to sow future seeds of victory in present defeat. You can lose a battle as a strategy to win an overall war.

NECESSARY LOSSES

Remember, you can lose a battle as part of a long-term plan.

Defeat is an opportunity to become stronger. Losing a battle actually teaches us how to win. If life was without defeat, victory would be meaningless.

Two steps forward, one step backward still marches you towards final victory.

KNOW WHEN TO STOP
• •

Do not be seduced by victory nor unnerved by defeat.

Emperor Bonaparte taught us that the most dangerous time in war is after a victory. Why? Because the victor feels invincible, and in that feeling of invincibility, he takes things too far—ultimately losing everything that was won.

Going too far is just as bad as falling too short.

Sidenote: You are more susceptible to the emotional toll of defeat when your eyes are not set on long-term victory. Defeat is always temporary; it is always forgotten the moment you win again.

RESULTS OVER PROCESS

· ·

Envisioning your grand strategy is a vital skill. It allows you to use two gifts of the mind at once: logic and creativity.

Having the results of your grand strategy in mind makes it easier to control your emotions, because your vision is far-seeing and clear. Foresight removes the variable of surprise from any setbacks you may encounter.

We think about the results, not the process. The process will unfold naturally.

Think lightly of yourself
and deeply of the world.

—DOKKODO 4

RELY ON REALITY

• •

Your strategy should be rooted in reality, not emotion and not in the supernatural.

Keep your feet on the ground. Apply statistics, probability, and the law of averages to every part of your plan.

Hoping to be the 1 out of 8,000,000 that wins the lottery is unrealistic. He who accounts for a supernatural intervention in his circumstance the least, is the most realistic.

THE FOREST OR THE TREES

· ·

Never do something without an eye on your ultimate objective.

Don't lose sight of the forest for the trees. Your ultimate objective is the forest; the trees are meaningless distractions trying to steal your attention.

Don't go about your day aloof. Always think about what you are thinking about. Your thoughts and decisions: do they help or hurt your ultimate cause?

TIME WELL SPENT

••

Prioritize activities that will make you stronger tomorrow. If it doesn't make you Smart, Fit, or Financially Secure, it is probably a waste of time.

This principle should be practiced within the boundaries of morality, decency, and biblical principle.

Take a moment to imagine your ideal circumstances: Mentally, Physically, and Financially.

What can you do today, to make tomorrow align with your goals?

WHY YOU NEED A FIVE-YEAR PLAN

· ·

"He who says he can and he who says he can't are both usually right."

—CONFUCIUS

Ensure that you are "he who says he can" by planning your life in five-year intervals–no more, no less.

Think of clear, long-term objectives that give direction to all your actions, large and small. You'll know when to sacrifice a pawn and when to lose a battle in order to serve your long-term objectives.

This is the ultimate strategy for your long-term plan. It assures your thoughts and energies will not go to waste, and your decisions will not be counterproductive to your plan.

DEPTH AND WIDTH
•••

Today, you widen your perspective. Dig deep into the reality of your circumstances, not just their surfaces. Widen your view.

Things are always more than they seem. Always break down the composition of the people and problems you are dealing with.

Train your mind to think critically so you can break down situations, circumstances, and people's moods. The word for this is exegesis: a critical explanation or interpretation of subject matter.

HONESTY WITH YOURSELF

Look at the world through the eyes of your troubles.

Yes, sometimes we are victims of trouble. We don't look for trouble, it just finds us.

However, most times, we create our troubles through poor planning, poor decision-making and poor execution.

Only by being honest with yourself about your shortcomings can you sit at the table with reality.

PASS ON THE PAST

• •

Lose your preconceptions. Being mostly rooted in your past experiences, they are your hinderance.

Our thoughts and emotions are rooted in our past experiences. By continuously making decisions based on past experiences, we are stuck reliving our bad experiences in perpetuity.

Subsequently, we will be continuously hindered and never make progress.... on anything!

Be detached from desire
your whole life long.

—DOKKODO 5

WISDOM IN COUNSEL

••

Gain the support of other people in your grand strategy. There is wisdom in counsel.

Need to make a decision? Find three people who are wiser than you, and ask for their advice.

Follow the advice of the majority.

DAY 29
ERADICATE THE ROOTS
●●●

Sever the roots. Think hard and think deep. Do not take appearances for reality. Uncover the roots and plot to destroy them. End the problem with finality.

We deal with the problem, not the symptoms.

Find the roots of the issue. Usually, your troubles can all be traced to one or two roots.

Sever them, and everything else disappears.

THE INDIRECT ROUTE

••

Hannibal Barca invaded Rome but Rome didn't fight back. Instead, Rome invaded Carthage, which forced Hannibal to leave Rome and defend his home.

Your lesson here is to take the indirect route. Bypass the obvious strategy by placing yourself at least two steps ahead.

Ignore the low-hanging fruit.

CONTROL BEFORE SUBMISSION

· ·

Be dispassionate. When you react to your circumstances, you lose initiative and forfeit control.

You want to submit your circumstances. But before you can do that, you must control them.

If you're emotional, you are not in control. Whatever is causing you to be emotional, is! But emotions are temporary. Accept the feeling, let it pass, and forge ahead with detachment.

Do not regret your
mistakes but meditate
and learn from them.

—DOKKODO 6

THE ART OF UNPREDICTABILITY

• •

People tend to predict the actions of those who surround them. Preventing your enemy from understanding your actions gives you a huge advantage.

They cannot conquer what they cannot understand.

Practice the art of unpredictability by tuning in to what your enemy expects of you. When they expect a "no," say "yes"–when a "yes" is expected, say "no."

Control them by keeping them guessing, always.

SETBACKS ARE TEMPORARY

• •

Maintain control of your emotions, and plot several moves ahead. See the entire chessboard.

Never make a permanent decision based on a temporary setback.

Thomas Edison tried 999 unsuccessful materials and methods before finally inventing the lightbulb, on his 1000th attempt. If he had decided any of those 999 setbacks were permanent failures, the world would be a pretty dark place.

Long-term view, always!

WEAPONIZE EMOTIONS

Infect your enemy with emotion. Make him lose the initiative.

When you're emotional, you make mistakes.

When you're emotional, you prioritize short-term relief. In doing this, you surrender control to your circumstances, to chance, and to your opponent.

Strike what your opponent treasures most. This is the best way to make him emotional.

SCALE YOUR EFFORTS

A man who ceases his efforts where he should not, will cease them everywhere.

Setbacks are to be anticipated. Remember, Rome wasn't built in a day.

Treat each opportunity, whatever its size may be, with the highest regard. If it only moves you forward an inch, that's still one inch in the right direction.

If you cannot be faithful with a little, you cannot be faithful with a lot.

THE BATTLEFIELD OF THE MIND

Fight your adversity on a mental level. Do not fight it head on. Fight and defeat it in the battlefield of the mind.

Your enemy is your emotions. When you are emotional, you make mistakes in favor of your adversity. The victory you seek over your present situation can only be secured in the battlefield of your mind.

ANGER IS A SPY

If you want to know what your opponent is thinking, make him angry and he will tell you.

Anger is a tool that you use, judiciously.

Do not allow it to be an emotion that controls you.

Think of emotions as gateways to the subconscious. You wouldn't give your enemy the keys to your house, so don't give him the benefit of seeing you angry.

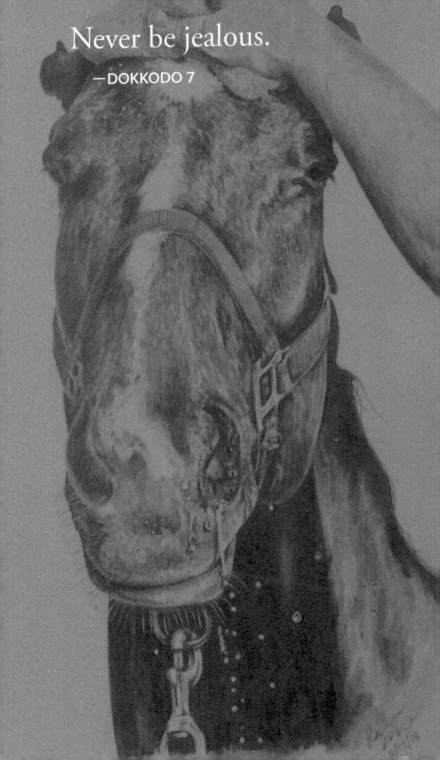

Never be jealous.

—DOKKODO 7

BUILD YOUR EXTRAPOLATION MUSCLE

••

Everyone has two sets of eyes. The eyes that see what is directly in front of you, and the eyes that discern the unseen.

Extrapolation is the greatest muscle you can develop. Strengthen it by meticulously observing the present.

Patterns are everywhere, if you look for them. What could they say about the future? Always account for wild cards.

Work backwards from future scenarios you envision, to inform your present action.

CONTEMPLATE YOUR STRENGTH

Conscientiousness is defined as being hard-working, orderly, responsible, thorough, self-controlled, and disciplined. It is the enemy of impulsivity.

Always contemplate your strength and resolve before engaging in battle.

No one builds a house before first counting the cost of that house. The last thing you want is to go into battle and find out you don't have the strength, resolve, or will to win.

Lay the blueprint of your house conscientiously, by setting realistic goals that protect your reserves.

CONTROL YOURSELF

••

Do not become angry. A disturbed mind is one you cannot control.

Anger is an emotion. Emotions are the mortal enemy of reason.

Control fires of emotion by bringing logic to them. Reason cools down any emotion.

CONTROL YOUR ENEMY
••

Make your enemy angry.

Acknowledge their accomplishments with detachment. Challenge them with facts. Exude a calm, level-headed demeanor when they try to appeal to your emotions.

A disturbed mind is unbalanced and easily controlled.

STRIKE FIRST AND STRIKE HARD

....

Be the first to act in any situation. Make your enemy emotional and unbalanced.

After your first strike? Strike even harder.

The mind is strong when it is prepared. Strike unexpectedly, so your enemy's emotions are in control of them.

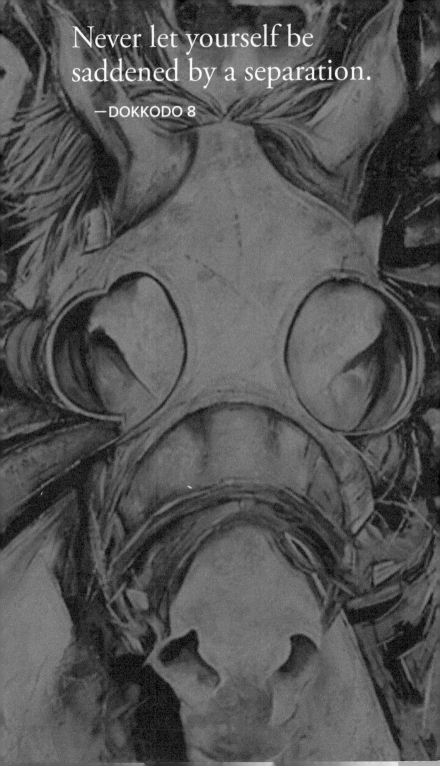

Never let yourself be saddened by a separation.

—DOKKODO 8

KNOW YOUR WEAKNESSES

· ·

Misfortune tends to attack where you have made no provisions.

Always tend to your weaknesses in life: Mental, Emotional, Financial.

Be honest with yourself about these shortcomings. Work on them and make them stronger. This way you can absorb whatever blow misfortune may try to give you.

CRAFTING YOUR FIVE-YEAR PLAN

•••

You will reach your destination with courage and a five-year plan.

When making your five-year plan, account for these intervals:

- Years one and two will consist of preparation. Think of these years as setting up your chess board.

- Years three and four will consist of execution. You will not see any fruit other than the progress of your plan during this time.

- Year five is when you will begin to see fruit and reach your destination.

Resentment and complaint
are appropriate neither
for oneself or others.

—DOKKODO 9

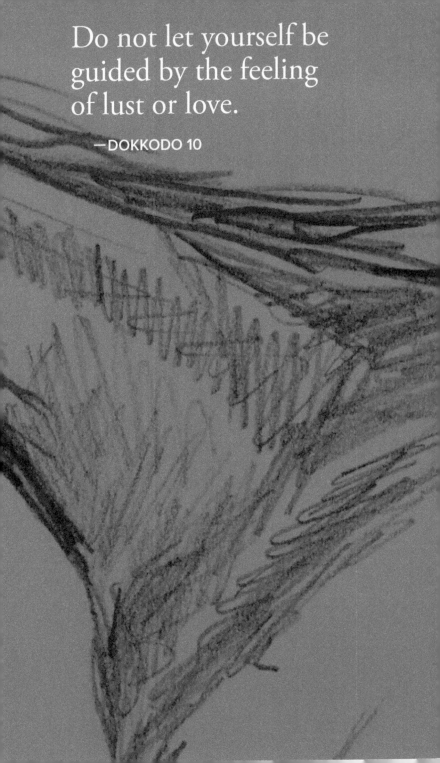

Do not let yourself be
guided by the feeling
of lust or love.

—DOKKODO 10

SLOW DELIBERATE ACTION

. . . .

"Slow in deliberation and swift in execution."

—NAPOLEON BONAPARTE

Remember the lesson from a month ago:

Humanity is very impatient, and stupidity is very bold… Don't charge ahead, WAIT!

Take a moment to reflect on the past 30 days. In what areas of your life do still lack restraint? See to it that you tighten every loose screw. Pause before every important decision today.

Between stimulus and response, there is time.

DAY 46
SET THEM UP TO FALL DOWN
••

Corner your opponent mentally before you trap them physically.
Inflict them with emotion so you can control their mood and
mindset.

Use truth as a weapon. Nothing cuts someone down like the truth.

An emotional opponent is a defeated opponent.

THE ART OF CONTROL

· ·

Keep your enemy operating on weakness:

A) Be aggressive.
B) Keep them on the defensive.
C) Do this by keeping them emotional.

Shift the Battlefield:

D) Shift your enemy into positions unfamiliar to them.

Compel mistakes:

E) Be elusive and deceptive.
F) Frustrate them so they make mistakes.
G) Do this by making them emotional.

THE IMPORTANCE OF THE FIRST MOVE

••

Striking first gives you control and allows you to set the pace.

The first move in a chess game sets the tone for the game.

No great war has ever been won on the defensive side.

Always take the offensive position. This way, you control your victory from the beginning.

THE FUNCTION OF MISFORTUNE

··

> **"Little minds are tamed and subdued by** misfortune; but great minds rise above them."

> —WASHINGTON IRVING

Make use of everything you encounter. Lessons are everywhere, to the man with open eyes.

Even misfortunes can be used, to learn what to do next time. When one door closes, another door opens.

There is juice to be squeezed from every circumstance that comes into your life: good, bad, or otherwise.

Learn to arrange the pieces that come your way.

A NEW ORDER
• •

The creator of disorder is now the head of the new order.

Muscles are built by damaging existing tissue. The body rushes to repair the damaged tissue, creating new growth. This orderly process of the body stems from disorder.

If you learn to benefit from stress and disorder, you can create difficult times in order to grow stronger, while everyone else grows weaker. Out of their weakness and your strength, a new order will arise, and you will have the high ground.

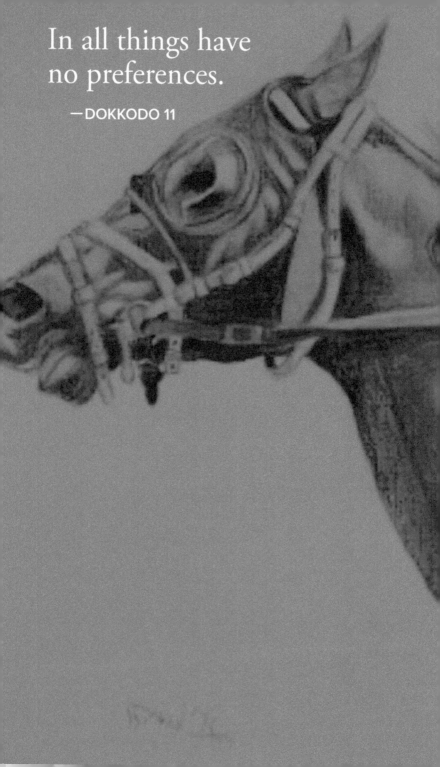

In all things have
no preferences.

—DOKKODO 11

SEIZE THE MOMENTUM
••

When you act before others, you seize the momentum.

Notice how people act in groups: 99% of the group will sit back and wait for a leader to emerge. In the end, the leader is 1% of the group.

Set the pace in your daily interactions.

Think of a group as a line of dominos. Each member makes the next one fall. When you are the first domino to set the chain in motion, you willfully control its disorder.

THE BULL OR THE BULLED

••

Make people react to you.

Create the circumstances.

You are either the bull, or you're getting bulled.

By creating circumstances, you manufacture the strings that are pulled. You are in control.

REJECT FEAR

· ·

Fear is your most debilitating emotion.

Fear is a liar. It is the weed that grows from the soil of worry.

Fear always exaggerates the unknown. Whatever consequences arise from your decisions, if any, won't be nearly as bad as you have been told they will.

Fear triggers your "fight or flight" instincts, which live in a small gland of the brain called the amygdala. The amygdala is obsessed with keeping you safe; it does not want you to step outside your comfortability box.

Fear handicaps your life.

REJECT ANGER

Control yourself, and your emotions. Getting angry and emotional will limit your options.

Anger will blind you to all the tools at your disposal, thereby limiting your choices about how to deal with a particular situation.

Remember: anger is only a feeling. Every emotion is temporary. Feelings are not facts.

COMBATTING MISFORTUNE

Do not engage in an exchange of punches with misfortune. Attack its support system instead.

Everything is cause and effect. What's holding up your poor financial situation? What continues to plague your relationships?

Attack the legs that misfortune stands on.

Eventually, it will crumble.

THE DANGER OF GOING TOO FAR

• •

Power is deceptive, in that it never shows its weakness.

Power makes you believe you are invincible. You lose all sense of balance and moderation, which leads you to take victories too far. In the process, you make yourself susceptible to Murphy's Law, and you are eventually defeated.

Do not let power strike you off balance. Going too far is just as bad as falling short. Live in the center.

"Let your moderation be known to all men."

—ST. PAUL

DAY 57
HIT WHERE IT HURTS

••

Attack what your enemy treasures the most.

A heart kneels before what it treasures.

When you attack what your enemy loves, it makes him emotional.
When he's emotional, his judgment is impaired.

You cannot war without a sound mind.

THE VALUE OF AN INDIRECT ATTACK

The only way to get a stubborn opponent to move is to attack them indirectly.

The Greeks won the Trojan war by hiding their entire army in a giant wooden horse, presented to the city of Troy as a gift. When the horse was hauled into the city, the Greeks decimated Troy from within.

Attack what your enemy treasures most. Forcing him to defend what he loves prevents him from mounting an offense against you.

Do not fight a war of attrition. Do not match strength for strength.

Be indifferent to
where you live.

—DOKKODO 12

THE CENTER PRINCIPLE

••

Occupy the central position everywhere you go, and in all that you do.

Make yourself the center of everything and everyone. This creates demand and dependency.

As long as you are the center, you will be needed.

Matter cannot exist without a nucleus.

RESPECT YOUR RESERVES

••

No plan survives contact with trouble. Knowing when to engage is just as important as combat itself.

If shots had been fired in the Cuban Missile Crisis, the Cold War could've escalated to total nuclear annihilation. Instead, the U.S. and Russia continued to build their arsenal reserves.

Simply put, your reserve is more important than both your plan and your attack. A strong reserve is to your plan what a strong foundation is to a home.

SOOTHE THE SAVAGE BEAST

• •

When dealing with a stubborn person, you need to separate them from their ties to the past. Rational arguments go nowhere with someone who is acting irrationally.

Our past experiences generally dictate how we think, present day. People will be easier to negotiate with after you soothe their past experiences.

Find common reference points first, then build your bridge from there.

THE MORE YOU KNOW
· ·

The more you know about someone, the more you can influence
their behavior.

Take time to observe the people around you. They will be too
obsessed with themselves to notice you're looking into their core.

Everyone has a weakness; often, their weaknesses will be very obvious. Pride, vanity, laziness, fear, and anger are common ones.

Ask questions and listen to the answers people give. Gain their trust,
then use it to your advantage. Every interaction is an opportunity to
advance.

Do not pursue the taste of good food.

—DOKKODO 13

THE ROOT OF WEAKNESS

• •

"If everyone is thinking alike, then somebody isn't thinking." — GENERAL GEORGE PATTON

Popular beliefs and opinions give great insight into weakness. People conform because it gives them the illusion of belonging. Fear of exclusion is the root of the desire to belong.

Dig deep into the weaknesses of those who surround you. This can be done easily, by making a five-column chart (one example of how to fill it in is provided):

POPULAR BELIEF/ OPINION	WHO HOLDS THIS BELIEF/ OPINION?	WHY DO THEY HOLD IT?	WHY IS HOLDING IT IMPORTANT?	WHAT IS THE ROOT OF THIS WEAKNESS?
It's important to have a flashy new car.	My boss and coworkers; celebrities	Desire to show power by external means	Fear of internal powerlessness	Vanity, Pride, Insecurity

Update your chart throughout the week. When you have a map, you can conquer the territory.

CONTROL THE CHAIN OF BEHAVIOR

··

The chain of behavior is shaped like a circle. It starts with a thought and it ends with a thought.

Thoughts impel actions, actions cause consequences, consequences cause beliefs about the situation. Beliefs are like thoughts, in that they are unseen–however, beliefs are backed by emotion as well as thought. If beliefs are not consciously considered, they produce habits that unconsciously shape character.

Character is both visible and invisible: it is demonstrated by visible action, and all actions start with invisible thoughts.

Control your character at the level of thought. Always ask yourself what you're thinking: is it a thought, or a belief?

APPEAL TO REASON < APPEAL TO EMOTION

••

To most people, on a subconscious level, reason is boring and emotions are exciting.

The general rule is to appeal to people on an emotional level. Doing this makes them easier to control.

People want to believe what you tell them, if you speak with authority. Start out by giving good news and compliments; it will make them excited to hear the next thing you have to say.

THE WEAKEST LINK

•••

A joint is the weakest part of a structure.

Emotions, beliefs, and opinions are the joints you must attack.

Use logic and discernment to understand what joins a person to the past and to others, or to a particular opinion.

This is imperative, if you want to get anywhere with a person who is stuck in a particular mindset or circumstance.

DAY 67
ANATOMY OF A LESSON
••

The longest way around is usually the shortest way home.

A lot of times we prolong bad situations by trying to remedy them.
Sometimes the only recourse is to ride out the storm.

God generally brings uncomfortable circumstances into your life
to teach you a lesson. The circumstance will not dissipate until you
learn the lesson it is designed to teach you. Though it may leave for a
time, it will always manifest itself later, in some other shape or form.

The lesson is designed to give you a skill that you will need for the
next level.

Some people never learn their lesson, usually in a particular part of
life–Money, Love, Friendship, for example–and live regressed in this
area their entire life. You have a chance to learn; take it.

SOFT TARGETS

• •

Never force a frontal battle. Attack the soft targets; these are what your enemy holds most dearly.

There are two methods of battle: direct and indirect. "In all fighting, the direct method may be used for joining battle, but indirect methods will be needed in order to secure victory," says Sun Tzu.

Soft targets are the backbone of the indirect method. When you hit these first, you make the enemy vulnerable.

Remember how Rome forced Hannibal Barca to defend the soft target of his home, by indirectly invading Carthage.

Do not hold on to possessions you no longer need.

—DOKKODO 14

AVOID DIRECT ATTACKS

• •

A direct attack will always strengthen your enemy's resolve.

Frontal approaches provoke stubborn resistance.

Remember this next time you think about trying to change someone's mind by telling them they're wrong.

Instead, change their mind indirectly, by telling them what they want to hear.

After you have gained their trust, dismantle their resistance from the inside.

THE POWER OF SUGGESTION

· ·

Always use more and more indirection. Never explain yourself.
Avoid straightforward answers.

In a world where we have no privacy, this is invaluable. People fear
what they cannot understand.

Harness the power of suggestion. If someone asks you a question,
answer it with a question.

FORCE THEM TO ADMIT DEFEAT

•••

Before Alexander the Great, the common military tactic was to invade a city in a direct attack. Alexander created a much more effective method of expanding his empire: he stationed troops on enemy grounds. The troops became friendly with the townspeople, but they also stood on every city corner, ready to rampage the town at a moment's notice.

This indirect tactic confused Alexander's enemies and wore them down mentally and emotionally. He gave them no choice but to admit defeat.

You must make your enemy acknowledge defeat from the bottom of his heart.

Otherwise, you will soon find him emboldened again, and yourself at war.

TOTAL ENVELOPMENT

Create pressure from all sides. The power of envelopment is ultimately psychological.

This is useful in everything, especially in dating.

For example, the Five Love Languages: words of affirmation, physical touch, receiving gifts, quality time, acts of service.

Women generally speak two of them, a primary and secondary. Speak all five to her and envelop her psychologically.

Mental submission comes before emotional and physical submission.

PINPOINT YOUR ATTACK

••

Put your target in a position of weakness before battle, so that victory is quick and easy.

The best position of weakness is a disturbed and anxious mind.

Study your target. What makes them emotional? Attack that.

Do not act following
customary beliefs.

—DOKKODO 15

PROBLEMS VS. DILEMMAS

Problems can be solved, dilemmas cannot.

A problem is a circumstance you can find a solution for. A dilemma is a circumstance where the only solutions are bad choices.

Think many steps ahead, sewing future seeds of victory in your current situation to avoid dilemmas for yourself.

STRATEGIC PLANNING

••

Craft a plan with options:

A) Give yourself room to move.

B) Give dilemmas, not problems.

C) Create maximum disorder.

The emphasis here is on C.

Disorder creates emotions, and emotions cloud judgment. When you cannot think clearly, you make mistakes.

FLOAT LIKE A BUTTERFLY, STING LIKE A BEE

• •

Stay mobile and stay elusive.

Involve yourself in many projects. Withhold details about your personal life. Keep everyone at arm's distance.

Moving targets are hard to hit.

This will also help you create interest with the people you interact with. Mystery creates curiosity.

PLAN FOR MISFORTUNE

••

Remember to factor bad luck into your planning. It is an art to absorb bad news gracefully–an art you must master.

If your reserves are down, you are more likely to react emotionally to trouble. Accounting for misfortune in your plan gives you freedom to react in a measured way.

Your reserve is more important than your attack, because it is with your reserve that you will outmaneuver bad luck.

THE VALUE OF PREPARATION

••

Victory depends on preparation and hard work. Without preparation, you are walking into battle unarmed.

No plan survives contact with trouble.

For this reason, you must have a plan B and C.

Do not collect weapons or practice with weapons beyond what is useful.

—DOKKODO 16

NEGOTIATING YOUR VICTORY

Always place yourself in a position of authority. Negotiate while advancing. Create an atmosphere of pressure, to ensure the enemy settles on your terms.

The enemy does not want to admit defeat; they will try to use indirect strategies on you, to get more than they deserve. Do not be fooled by these appeals, which are designed to play on your morals.

The more you take, the more you can give back in meaningless concessions while negotiating.

THE END JUSTIFIES THE MEANS

Trust is not a matter of ethics. Trust is a maneuver; a quality that is for sale.

I wish this wasn't true, but it is.

You should not be bound to any moral or ethical codes of conduct. The end justifies the means.

Sidenote: This is the general rule in this unforgiving world that we live in. The exceptions to this rule are the people that you love and cherish.

SAVE YOURSELF THE HEADACHE

• •

Know what you want and what people around you are capable of giving. Don't expect to move mountains in a single step, and don't expect greatness from mediocre people. This will only give you a headache in the end—or worse, it will set you up for disaster.

Remember the myth of Icarus: he was given a set of wings and warned not to fly too close to the sun. Once he was in the air, his emotions got the best of him, and he flew so high that the sun melted his wings. He fell into the sea and drowned.

Honor your wings by preparing for the flight.

Know the people around you. Don't ask for more than they are capable of giving.

RISKING VS. GAMBLING

· ·

When are you risking and when are you gambling?

You can recover from a risk, but you cannot recover from a gamble. How do you know the difference?

Risk originates in your gut or your mind. A gamble originates in your emotions.

Risks are mentally calculated. Gambles are emotionally calculated.

Do not fear death.

—DOKKODO 17

THE ARMOR OF ELUSIVENESS
••

The less people understand you and where you are headed, the more room you have to maneuver.

Familiarity breeds contempt, and contempt gives headaches. Your mind is your most valuable asset; protect it accordingly.

The less you say the better. The less people know about you the better. Coldness is the general rule.

DEFEAT VS. DISASTER

. . . .

Short-term defeat is better than long-term disaster.

You can easily recover from a defeat. It will be very difficult to recover from disaster.

Better to deal with the discomfort of treating a small tumor than to let it spread throughout the body.

Today, take an x-ray of your life. Swiftly eradicate any tumors.

INTEGRITY AND PERSEVERANCE

Do not start what you do not have the heart or intention to finish.

Every great warrior has integrity and perseverance.

Integrity is a quality of being complete and undivided. Perseverance is the continued effort to achieve something despite difficulties, failure, or opposition.

Either have the integrity to not attempt it, or the perseverance to see it through until the end.

BEWARE OF BIG WINS

•••

The most dangerous time to make a decision is after a big win. Victory makes you feel invincible in the same way defeat makes you feel hopeless.

Hopelessness and invincibility are just two emotional states. Resist the temptation to identify with these emotions.

When you feel invincible, you tend to overextend yourself. In the process, you lose everything you gained.

EVERYTHING IS TEMPORARY

••

Victory and defeat are temporary. Everything except death is a transition.

Approach victory and defeat as two sides of the same coin. Each produce a strong emotional reaction; neither determines the future. Emotions want to trick you into believing they are permanent states of mind.

The best thing you can do is sow future seeds of victory in your present victory or defeat. Every battle won or lost isn't the end, but the start.

ONLY THE END

· ·

People never regard how something started or what happened in the process. Only the end of a thing is important.

Statistics from Stanford indicate that negative impressions caused by bad publicity diminish over time. In fact, in the end, negative publicity is just as effective as positive publicity, because it creates awareness.

Human are results-oriented. What happens on the way to victory or defeat doesn't matter; people will not remember. All they will concern themselves with is the final outcome.

Do not seek to possess
either goods or fiefs
for your old age.

—DOKKODO 18

CONTROL REALITY

••

If you control the perception of reality, then you control the people.

Our brains are wired to react to the seen, not the unseen. The use of media by tyrants and government is a great demonstration of this principle.

What is perceived (unseen) is not necessarily real (seen). Over time, as enough perceptions are vocalized, the unseen becomes reality.

Use this knowledge like armor and a sword.

Beware of unseen forces that are trying to influence you—this is your armor. See to it that others perceive you as a formidable opponent—this is your sword.

THE ART OF DECEPTION

· ·

"Appear weak when you are strong, and strong when you are weak."

—SUN TZU

Deception mirrors reality. Lies are merely negations of truth.

Deceive your enemy by appearing clueless and unorganized, then blow them out of the water with your preparation and strategy.

What is false will mirror what is true, making it ambiguous and difficult to tell reality from make believe.

THE ELEMENT OF SURPRISE

No one is so brave that they are not disturbed by the unexpected.

The element of surprise is a power tool. It will make people emotional, and when they are emotional, they are weak.

Some of the most devastating battles in history were won by a surprise attack strategy.

Study the people around you. The more you know about what they expect from you, the easier it is to catch them off guard.

KNOW YOUR ENEMY

••

Do not get caught by surprise or you will lose your discipline and security.

Think of every possible reaction that the enemy can have to your action. Cover your bases.

One of the biggest mistakes you can make is to assume your enemy thinks similarly to you. If you do this, you are likely to misfire.

Watch him in a calculated manner; get to know his strategy. Tune in to subtle signals he sends about his true motives.

Respect God without
counting on his help.

—DOKKODO 19

LIVE BY REASON

· ·

The great warrior, Achilles, had one weak spot: his heel. He was undefeated in battle until a tricky opponent sliced his heel with a sword.

Do not let your emotions overwhelm your strategy. Emotions are always the weak spot; they are the heel that can lead to ruin.

Your strategy was conceived in reason. Reason trumps emotions. Do not allow your emotions to cloud your judgment. Live by reason; bring logic to your emotions, so you can plan around them.

LESS IS MORE

Anything that has a form can be attacked. Learn to conceal yourself in nothingness.

Keep your plans secret. Keep your thoughts secret. Keep your emotions secret.

What cannot be discerned cannot be conquered.

MINIMIZE MURPHY'S LAW

· ·

In most conflicts, time is the problem, because it brings Murphy's Law into play.

Be slow to deliberate and quick to execute.

Life is a cycle of action and inaction. Use time to your advantage. If you've prepared sufficiently, it's time to act!

When you work with time, and not against it, you cultivate resilience and fortitude.

Resilience and fortitude minimize the negative effects of Murphy's Law.

THE WAR OR THE LOSS

· ·

What will cost you more: the War or the Loss?

Sometimes the prize is not worth the chase.

Opportunities can be misleading. Not everything requires your involvement.

Carefully assess the risks involved, before committing to a project. Sometimes deferral is the wiser choice. Turning down an offer may also surprise your enemies.

You may abandon your own body but you must preserve your honor.

—DOKKODO 20

SOW SEEDS OF DOUBT

· ·

Do not implant ideas; rather, unearth doubts.

Doubt is a product of fear, and fear is one of man's greatest weaknesses.

If you want a person to embrace your idea, don't mention it to him. Instead, sow seeds of doubt into his mind about his plan. This will entice him to ask for your advice.

ENVISION THE END RESULT

Think in terms of the end result.

When you envision the outcome, your brain automatically begins to discern ways to make it happen.

Don't get lost in the details. It's important to be specific in your planning, but trouble can always intervene. Roll with the punches. Trust your ability to reason as you conquer each task.

If you focus on the process, you'll quickly go weary. Think of the end result, and you'll stay motivated throughout the process.

THE NATURE OF LESSONS

••

Most things are not evils, but paternal corrections from God.

There is a lesson to learn in every difficulty. It is God trying to father you.

St. Paul tells us that God determines **all** things according to the counsel of his will.

Embrace all the good and evil that befalls you; they are lessons and tests designed to ready you for the next level.

ETERNAL WISDOM

....

"**Employ your time in improving your-**self by other men's writings, so that you shall gain easily what others have labored hard for."

—SOCRATES

Through the lives of Great men, you can learn much. Read their writings. Doing so is like asking their spirits for advice.

Place yourself in the company of greatness. Make the story of your life one worth reading.

Never stray from the way.

—DOKKODO 21